UNDER THE TABLE AND DREAMING

Cover photography by Stuart Dee
Photography © C. Taylor Crothers unless otherwise noted

CONTENTS

Dave Matthews Band

DAVE MATTI

John Falls

There was a time when every rock 'n' roll movement sprung from the grass roots. While much has changed in the music industry over the years, a band working entirely on its own—outside the parameters of current trends—can generate the kind of organic electricity that marketers spend a fortune trying to create. Case in point: Charlottesville, Virginia's Dave Matthews Band.

In the four years since Matthews put together the genre-blending quintet, the band's charged live performances have consistently attracted packed clubs, theatres and arenas across the country. "It's been a very natural, very low-key progression," Dave says. "I don't feel like we've had this drastic, overnight success. It's basically been a matter of word-of-mouth—people liking what they've seen and bringing some friends with them the next time around."

Those die-hard fans have also snapped up copies of the band's self-released debut, *Remember Two Things* (over 250,000 copies sold since its fall 1993 release), on their Bama Rags Records label—a remarkable feat, considering the album was independently distributed. And while the band notes that the first release may have hinted at their potential, they are satisfied that their major-label debut, *Under The Table And Dreaming*—produced by Steve Lillywhite (U2, Talking Heads, Rolling Stones)—captures the nuances of their edgy musical amalgam and intricate interplay of the band's exceptional live persona. The critical praise for the album has since been exhaustive; *Rolling Stone* called it "one of the most ambitious releases" of 1994.

With singer/guitarist Matthews' expressive voice at the fore, the band—reedman LeRoi Moore, violinist Boyd Tinsley, bassist Stefan Lessard and drummer Carter Beauford—weaves a mesh of sounds that has been described as "unpeggable and totally addictive." Each member showcases a highly individual approach to his instrument, making the band a truly unique and eclectic ensemble.

"The way I look at it, we have five lead voices in this band," Dave continues. "I may be the first thing people notice, since I do the singing, but there are times when LeRoi's sax is the voice, and times when Boyd's violin is at the front. And in Carter and Stefan, we have something that goes far beyond a simple rhythm section. There are very few times when the audience has just one thing to listen to."

A glimpse at the 12 songs comprising *Under The Table And Dreaming* imparts the obvious: that the band is flourishing on its own musical terms, and in the process has veered far away from the susceptibility of new bands to being pigeonholed. On *Under The Table*, evocative melodies soar over compact grooves on the likes of "Satellite" and "Jimi Thing," while the band airs its more visceral nature on rockers like "Rhyme & Reason" and "What Would You Say." Such stylistic shifts occur within songs as well; the propulsive "Warehouse" boasts a richly-textured fusion-style break, while "Ants Marching" melds straight-up funk and a lively, high-lonesome bluegrass fiddle.

"In the beginning, I didn't have a fully formed idea of what I was going for," Dave admits. "I just set out to assemble my dream group of musicians—people I'd been listening to locally for years—and much to my surprise, they all agreed to join. And even after all this time, we still work the same way. There are no rules in this band, no one to say, 'Wait, you can't do that.'" With its absolute refusal to recognize borders and limitations, the Dave Matthews Band possesses the kind of musical chops and vision that the *San Francisco Chronicle* praised as "a means of expression free enough of cliché to be an authentic alternative."

Dave Matthews Band

DAVE SPEAKS OUT

The Best Of What's Around

Thanks to bad days and hard times, we notice the sweet nectar.

What Would You Say

A dog, a stuffed monkey and a television with 400 channels.

Satellite

We're awed by the wonders of technology. The accomplishments we've made to bring us closer together by plane, road or satellite are fantastic. What I fear most is that while we play with our toys and technologies, we forget from where our playfulness comes.

Rhyme & Reason

No rhyme . . .
no reason.

Typical Situation

Insert the last line of the
book *Animal Farm* and
attribute it to the author.

Dancing Nancies

What if you weren't
reading this?

Ants Marching

I love ants. We share a lot
with them . . . but they
are less talk.

LeRoi Moore

Carter Beauford

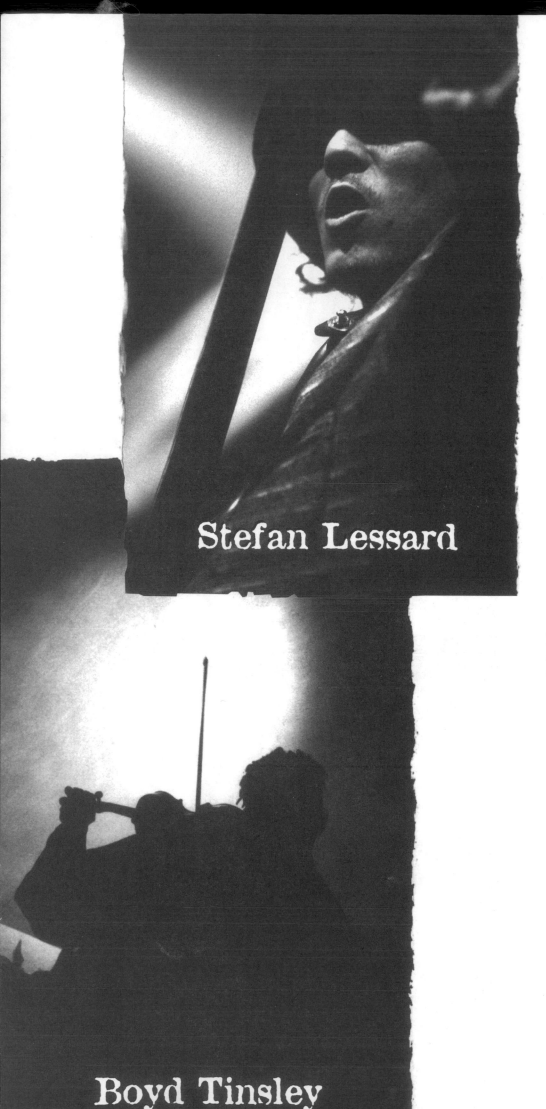

Stefan Lessard

Boyd Tinsley

Lover Lay Down

Careful with that word "love."

Jimi Thing

In England it's a condom.

Warehouse

Have you ever been in you grandparents' attic?

Pay For What You Get

I spend a lot of time thinking about what I don't have and how I can get it. When I succeed in attaining it, often it comes with things I didn't expect.

#34

For Miguel Valdez.

The Best Of What's Around

Words and Music by David Matthews

Would you say— you're feel - ing— low? And— so—— a good—

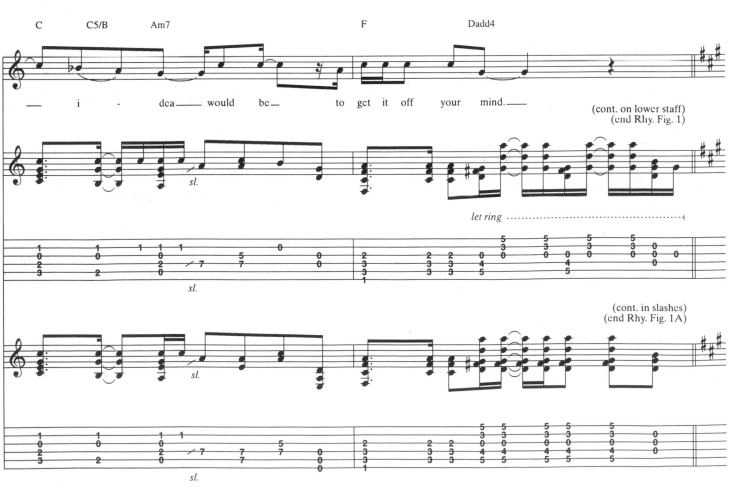

— i - dea—— would be— to get it off your mind.——

(cont. on lower staff)
(end Rhy. Fig. 1)

let ring

(cont. in slashes)
(end Rhy. Fig. 1A)

Additional Lyrics

2. And if you hold on tight to what you think is your thing,
You may find you're missing all the rest.
Well, she run up into the light surprised.
Her arms are open. Her minds's eye is...

2nd Chorus:
Seeing things from a better side than most can dream.
On a clearer road I feel, oh, you could say she's safe.
Whatever tears at her, whatever holds her down.
And if nothing can be done, she'll make the best of what's around. *(To Bridge)*

What Would You Say

Words and Music by David Matthews

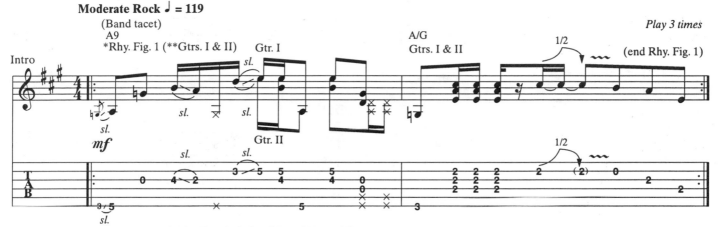

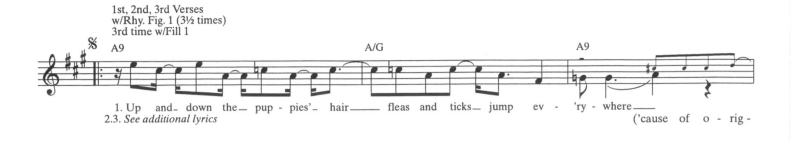

1st, 2nd, 3rd Verses
w/Rhy. Fig. 1 (3½ times)
3rd time w/Fill 1

1. Up and down the pup-pies' hair fleas and ticks jump ev-'ry-where ('cause of o-rig-
2.3. *See additional lyrics*

Down the hill fell Jack and Jill, and

i - nal sin).

2nd & 3rd times Gtrs. I & II substitute Rhy. Fig. 1A

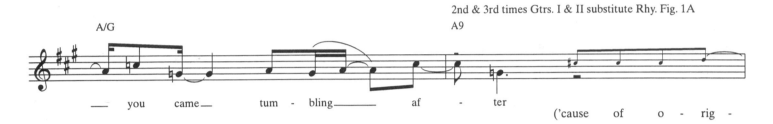

you came tum - bling af - ter ('cause of o-rig-

i - nal sin).

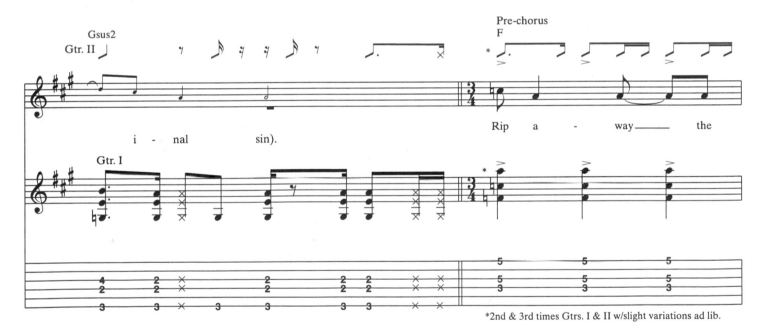

Rip a - way the

*2nd & 3rd times Gtrs. I & II w/slight variations ad lib.

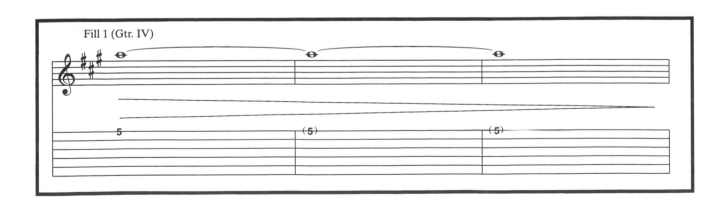

Fill 1 (Gtr. IV)

Ev - 'ry___ dog has its day, ev - 'ry___ day has its way of be - ing for -

got - ten.   *Mom, it's my birth - day.   Would you say,___ hey?

*Lead vocal is doubled by bkgd. vocals, next 5 bars.

(Now, what would you   say?)___

What___ would you   say?___

*w/crowd noises

*Till 5th bar of Sax solo

*Substitute muted strings for octaves in parentheses, 1st time only.

*Gtr. I to left of slashes in TAB.

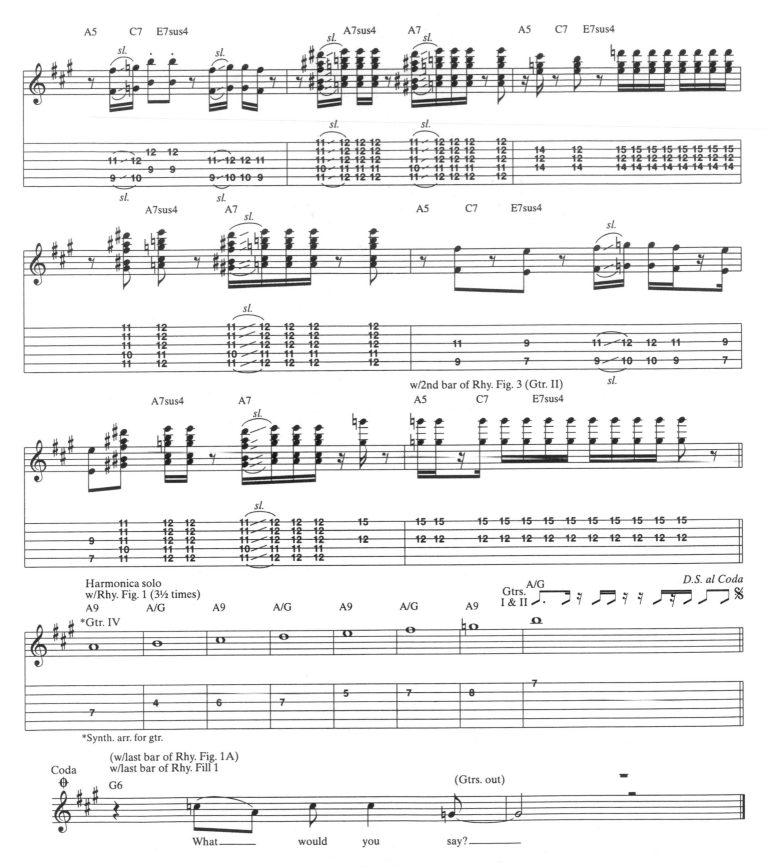

Additional Lyrics

2.3. I was there when the bear ate his head, thought it was a candy.
  (Everyone goes in the end.)
  Knock, knock on the door. Who's it for? There's nobody in here.
  (Look in the mirror, my friend.)

2nd, 3rd Pre-chorus:
  I don't understand, at best, and cannot speak for all the rest.
  The morning rise, a lifetime's passed me by.
   What would you say?

Satellite

Words and Music by David Matthews

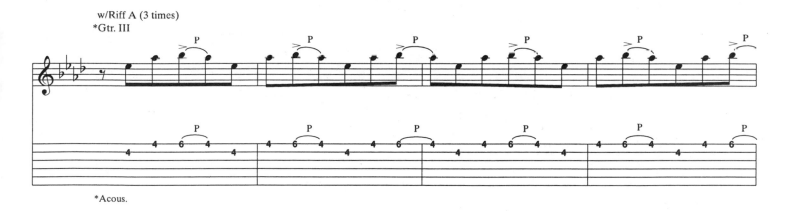

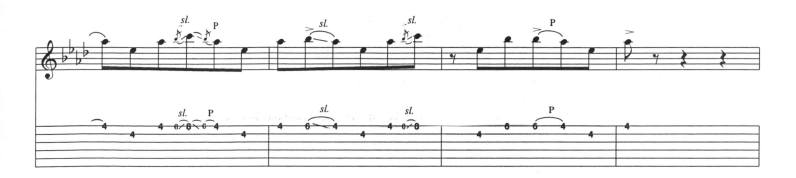

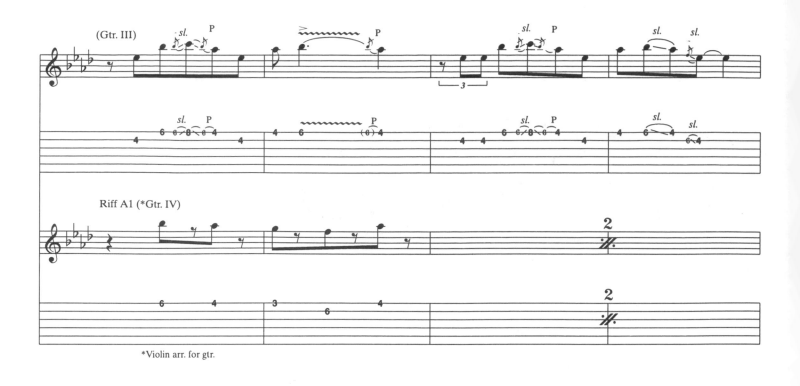

*Violin arr. for gtr.

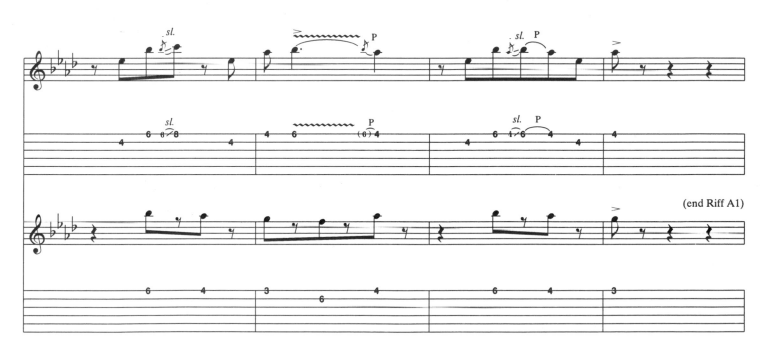

1st, 2nd, 3rd Verses
w/Riff A (1¾ times)
2nd time w/Riff A1 (1¾ times) & Riff B
3rd time w/Riff A1 (1 time only)

N.C.

(1.3.) lite   in   my   eyes,_____   like   a   dia - mond   in   the   sky.
(2.)   lite   head - lines read._____ Some - one's se - crets you've seen, eyes___ and

*Harmony is sung 3rd time only.

How   I   won - der.   Sat - el - lite   strong__ from __ the __ moon,—
ears__ have been.   Sat - el - lite   dish__ in __ my yard,—

and   the   world   your__ bal - loon. Peep - ing__ Tom__ for   the__
tell   me   more,   tell__ me__ more. Who's__ the__ king__ of   your__

Riff B (*Gtr. V)   Play 3 times

w/slide

*Acous.

Play 3 times   (Gtr. V out)

*Vib. w/slide.

23

w/Riff A1 (last 4 bars only)

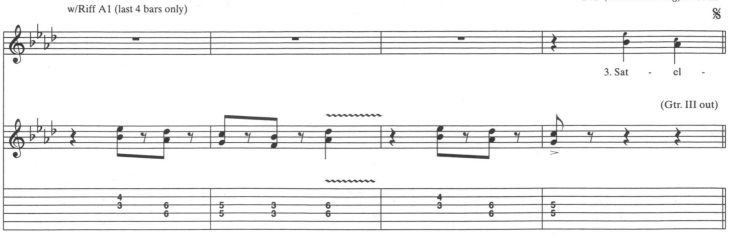

Coda

w/Riffs A & D1
N.C.

eyes._____

Gtr. V

w/slide

w/Riff A1 (last 4 bars only)

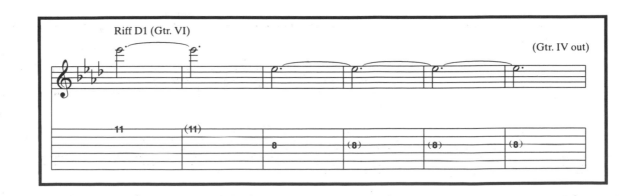

Riff D1 (Gtr. VI)

(Gtr. IV out)

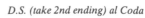

Rhyme & Reason

Words and Music by David Matthews

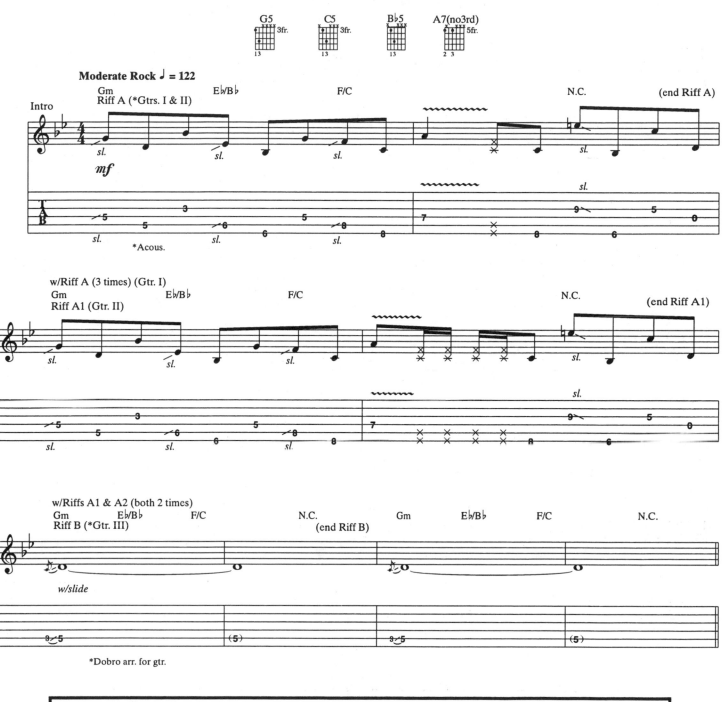

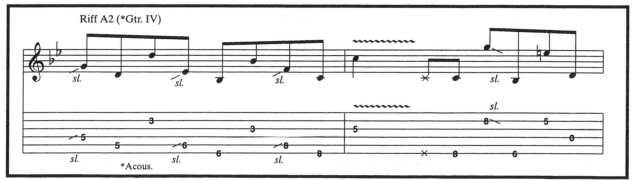

es ___ must be __ my __ soul. ___ I've had e - nough, I've__

___ had e - nough of be - ing a - lone. ___ I've got __ no place to __ go. ____

Chorus
w/Rhy. Figs. 1 & 1A (both 4 times)
**w/Gtr. III ad lib

___ My head won't leave my head a - lone, __ and I don't be - lieve __ it will__ un - til I'm__

*Omit slur on D.S.
**1st time next 16 bars,
2nd time next 24 bars.

___ dead__ and __ gone. My head won't leave my head a - lone, and I don't be - lieve__

__ it will__ un - til I'm__ six feet__ un - der__ ground ____

To Coda

__ in __ my grave. Ly - ing,__ wired shut__ and

qui - et in__ my grave.__ Leave_ me here. Leave_ it__ to_ me to_ waste

33

36

Typical Situation

Words and Music by David Matthews

Moderately ♩ = 100

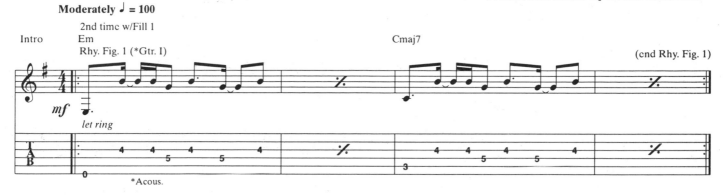

Intro
2nd time w/Fill 1
Em
Rhy. Fig. 1 (*Gtr. I)

Cmaj7

(end Rhy. Fig. 1)

mf   *let ring*   *Acous.*

1st, 4th Verses
w/Rhy. Fig. 1 (3 ¾ times)
1st time w/Fill 2

Em   Cmaj7

1. Ten fin - gers___ count - ing we have___ each.___ Nine plan - ets___
4. *See additional lyrics*

1st time w/Fill 3
Em

a - round the sun___ re - peat.___ Eight- ball___ the last___ if___ you tri - um - phant be.___

Cmaj7   1st time w/Fill 3
                                          Em

Sev - en o - ceans___ pum - mel___ the shores of___ the sea.___ It's a ty - pi - cal sit - u - a -

2nd time w/Fill 5   Cmaj7

tion in___ these typ - i - cal___ times.___ Too man - y choic - es,___ hey yeah.

Fill 1 (*Gtr. II)

rake

Clean elec.

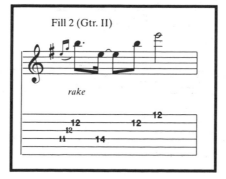

Fill 2 (Gtr. II)

rake

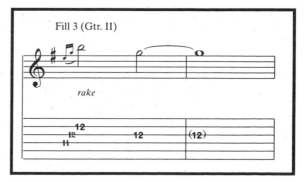

Fill 3 (Gtr. II)

rake

1st time w/Fill 4   2nd time w/Fill 5

It's a typ-i-cal sit-u-a-tion in these typ-i-cal times. Too man-y

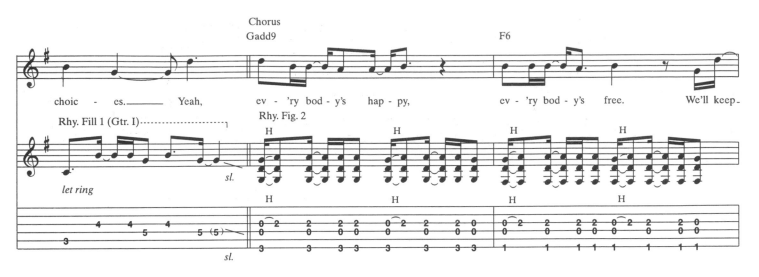

Chorus

choic-es. Yeah, ev-'ry bod-y's hap-py, ev-'ry bod-y's free. We'll keep

the big door o-pen. Ev-'ry-one-'ll come a-round.

(end Rhy. Fig. 2)

w/Rhy. Fig. 2

Why are you dif-f'rent? Why are you that way?

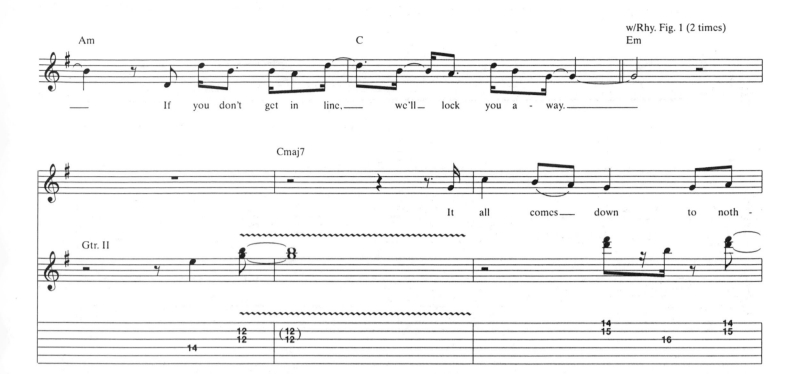

If you don't get in line, we'll lock you a - way.

It all comes down to noth -

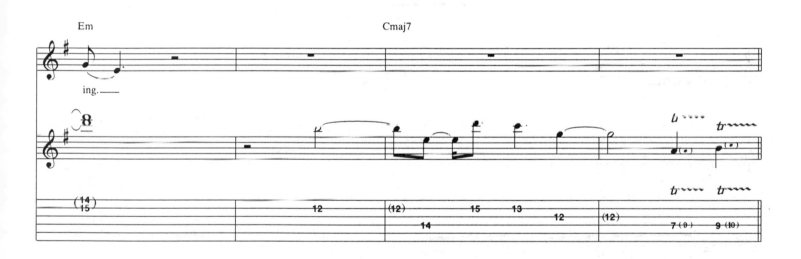

ing.

2. Six senses feeling five a - round a sense
3. *See additional lyrics*

(Play 1st time only)

*Next 6 bars

Additional Lyrics

3. We can't do a thing about it.
   Too many choices, hey yeah.
   It's typical situation in these typical times.
   Too many choices. *(To Chorus)*

4. It's a typical situation in these typical times.
   Too many choices, hey yeah.
   It's typical situation in these typical times.
   Too many choices.
   We can't do a thing about it.
   Too many choices, hey yeah.
   It's a typical situation in these typical times.
   Too many choices.

Dancing Nancies

Words and Music by David Matthews

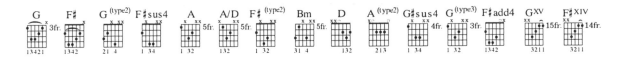

Moderately ♩ = 100

*Refers to both gtrs.
**Two acous. gtrs. arr. for one (throughout).

dant?___ Could I have_ been___ a mil-lion-aire in Bel Air?___ Could I have_ been___

___ lost some-where in Par-is?___ Could I have_ been___ your_ lit-tle broth-

er? Could I have___ been,___ oh, an-y-one oth-er than___ me? Could I have___ been,_

___ oh,___ an-y-one oth-er than___ me? Could I have been___ an-y-one oth-er than___

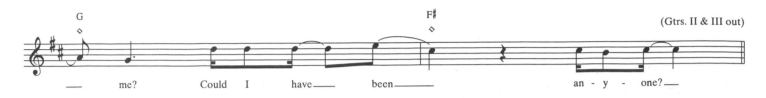

G (Gtrs. II & III out)

F#

— me? Could I have —— been —— an - y - one? —

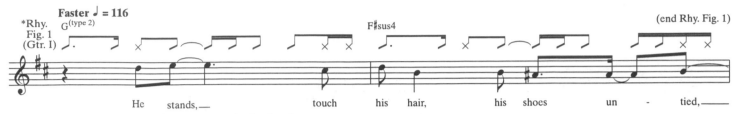

Faster ♩ = 116

*Rhy. Fig. 1 (Gtr. I)   G(type 2)   F#sus4   (end Rhy. Fig. 1)

He stands, —— touch his hair, his shoes un - tied, ——

*Throughout Rhy. Fig. 1, play only lowest note of chord on beat 1.
Play all rhy. figs. w/slight variations ad lib when recalled (throughout).

w/Rhy. Fig. 1 (2½ times)
G(type 2)   F#sus4   G(type 2)   F#sus4

—— tongue - gap - ing stare.. Could I have - been a mag - net —— for mon - ey? Could I have - been

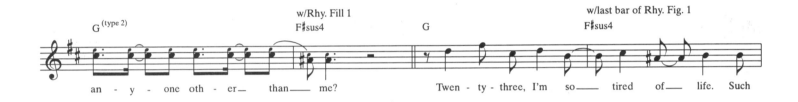

w/Rhy. Fill 1
G(type 2)   F#sus4   G   F#sus4   w/last bar of Rhy. Fig. 1

an - y - one oth - er —— than —— me?   Twen - ty - three, I'm so —— tired of —— life. Such

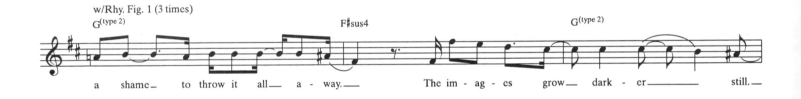

w/Rhy. Fig. 1 (3 times)
G(type 2)   F#sus4   G(type 2)

a shame — to throw it all —— a - way. —— The im - ag - es grow —— dark - er —— still.

F#sus4   G(type 2)   F#sus4   A
                                                                                           Gtr. I

—— Could I have - been an - y - one oth - er —— than —— me? And then I —— look up at the sky.

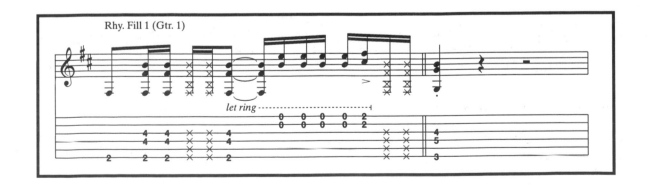

Rhy. Fill 1 (Gtr. 1)

let ring

44

Ants Marching

Words and Music by David Matthews

He wakes up on the morn - ing.___ Does___ his teeth, bite to eat and he's roll - ing. Nev - er chang - es___ a ___ thing.___ The week ends, the week ___ be - gins, ___ she thinks. We look at each oth - er, ___ won - d'ring what the oth - er is think - ing.___

Lover Lay Down

Words and Music by David Matthews

Jimi Thing

Words and Music by David Matthews

1. Late - ly I've been feel - in' low, a rem - e - dy is what I'm
2. See additional lyrics

seek - in'. I take a taste of what's be - low come a - way

*Play w/slight variations ad lib when repeated or recalled (throughout).

to some-thing bet-ter. What I___ want___ is what I've

not___ got but what I need___ is all a-round__ me.

Reach-ing, search-ing,___ nev-er stop and I'll say...___

If you___ could keep___ me float-ing just for a while___

*1st & 2nd times sing lower harmony only. 3rd time sing higher harmony only.

till I get___ to the end___ of this___ tun-nel, oh, { 1.2. Mom - my._____
                                                       3. Jim - i.

*Don't strike chord. Hammer on ④
while letting other stgs. ring.

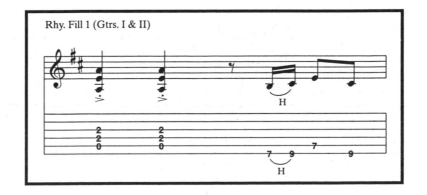

Rhy. Fill 1 (Gtrs. I & II)

If you_ could keep_ me float - ing just for a while,_____ I'll get_ back to_____ you.____

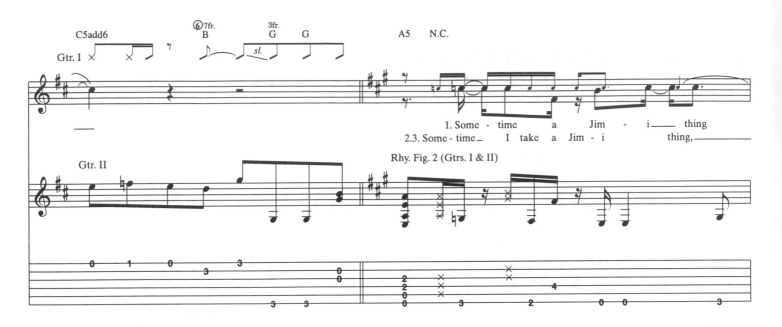

1. Some - time a Jim - i_____ thing
2.3. Some - time_ I take a Jim - i thing,_____

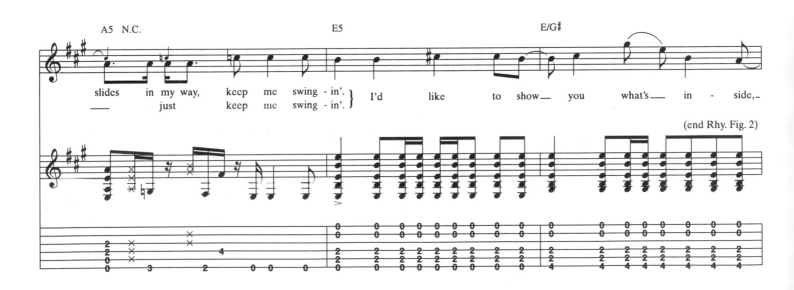

slides in my way, keep me swing - in'. } I'd like to show_ you what's_ in - side,_
_____ just keep me swing - in'.

_____ but I should - n't care_____ if you don't_ like_ it. Broth - er_____ cha - os_____

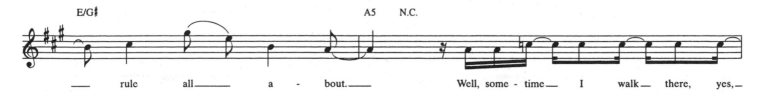

rule all a - bout. Well, some - time I walk there, yes,

God knows some - time I take a bus there. Should - n't care, I should - n't care, be - reaved

as I'm feel - in'.

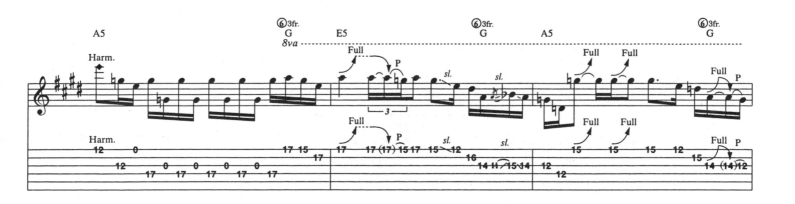

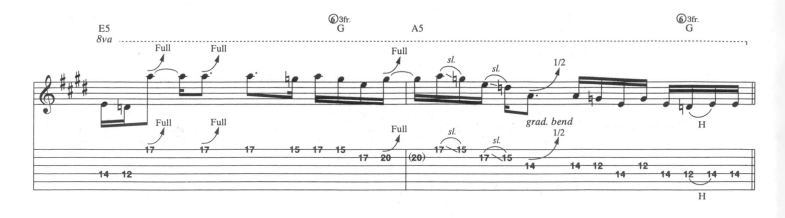

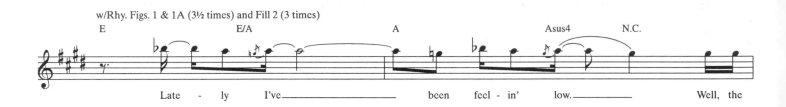

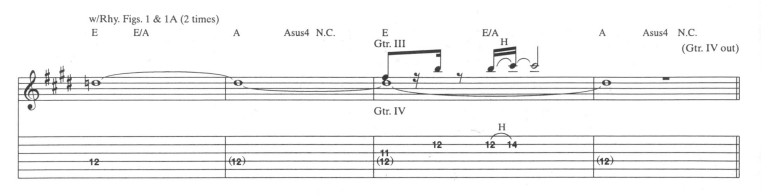

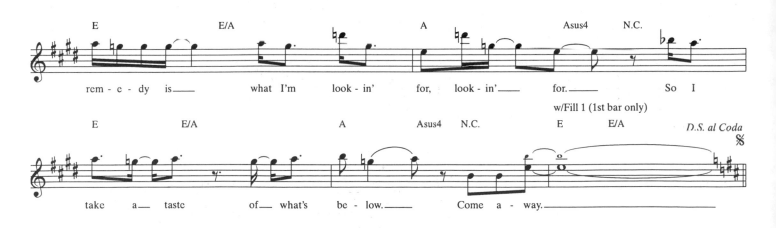

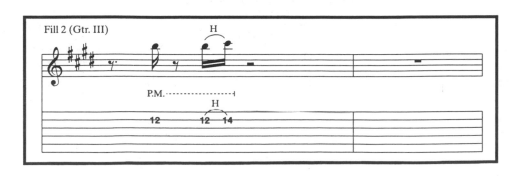

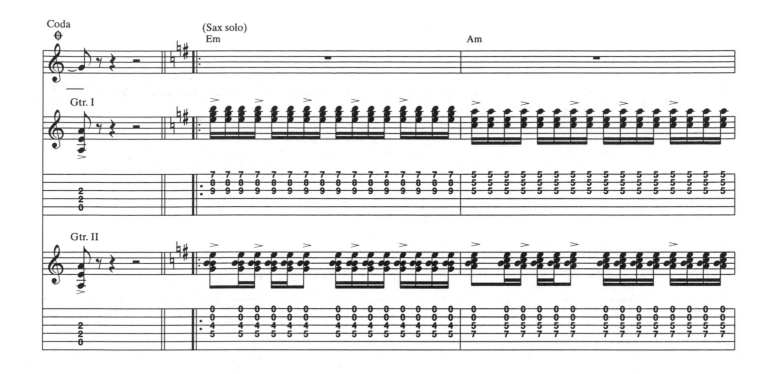

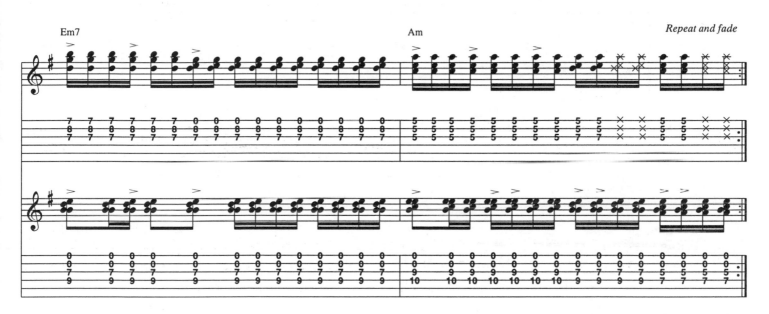

Additional Lyrics

2. The day is gone, I'm on my back
Starin' up at the ceiling.
I take a drink, sit back and relax.
Smoke my mind to make me feel better for a small time.
What I want is what I've not got
And what I need is all around me.
Reachin', searchin', never stop.
And I'll say...
If you keep me floating, *etc.*

Warehouse

Words and Music by David Matthews

Additional Lyrics

3. Hey, we have found
   Becoming one in a million.
   Slip into the crowd.
   This question I found in the gap in the sidewalk.

   2nd Pre-chorus:
   Keep all your sights on.
   Hey, the black cat changing colors.
   And you can walk under ladders.
   And swim as the tide choose to turn you. *(To Chorus)*

4. Shut up, I'm thinking.
   I had a clue, now it's gone forever.
   Sitting over these bones,
   You can read in whatever. You're needing to...

   3rd Pre-chorus:
   Keep all your sights on.
   Yeah, man, the black cat changing colors.
   When it's not the colours that matter,
   but that they'll all fade away.

   2rd Chorus:
   And I, life goes on.
   End of tunnel, TV set, spot in the middle.
   Static fade, statistical bit.
   Soon I'll fade away, I'll fade away.
   Oh, but this I admit.
   Seems so good, hard to believe an end to it.
   The warehouse is barc, nothing, it's all inside of it.
   The walls and halls have disappeared, they've disappeared. Well.
   My love, I'd love to stay here, *etc.*

Pay For What You Get

Words and Music by David Matthews

Sur - prise,— sur - prise.— You pay— for what— you get.— You pay—

— for what— you get.—

Ev - 'ry-bod - y asks— me how— she's do - ing. Has she

real - ly lost— her... Ev - 'ry-bod - y asks— me— how— she's—

— do - ing since she— went a - way.— I said,— "I

— could - n't— tell you, I'm— o - kay."— I'm

o - kay. I'm o - kay. How are you?

Pay—

#34

Music by David Matthews,
Leroi Moore, Carter Beauford
and Haines Fullerton

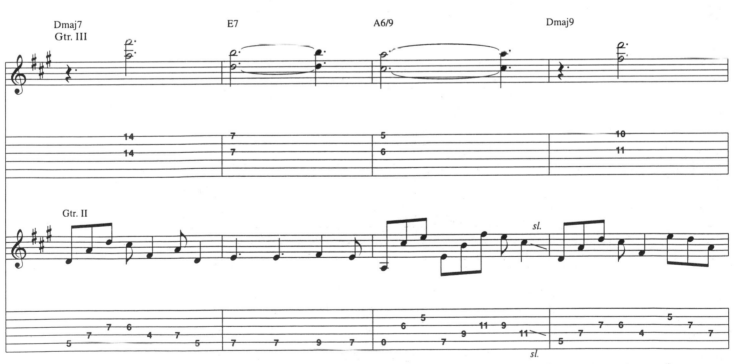

TABLATURE: A six-line staff that graphically represents the guitar fingerboard. By placing a number on the appropriate line, the string and fret of any note can be indicated. For example:

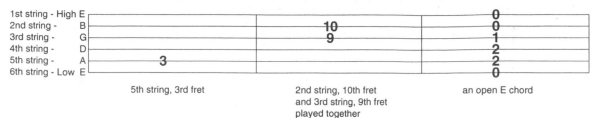

1st string - High E
2nd string - B
3rd string - G
4th string - D
5th string - A
6th string - Low E

5th string, 3rd fret

2nd string, 10th fret and 3rd string, 9th fret played together

an open E chord

Definitions for Special Guitar Notation

BEND: Strike the note and bend up ½ step (one fret).

BEND: Strike the note and bend up a whole step (two frets).

BEND AND RELEASE: Strike the note and bend up ½ (or whole) step, then release the bend back to the original note. All three notes are tied; only the first note is struck.

PRE-BEND: Bend the note up ½ (or whole) step, then strike it.

PRE-BEND AND RELEASE: Bend the note up ½ (or whole) step, strike it and release the bend back to the original note.

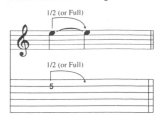

UNISON BEND: Strike the two notes simultaneously and bend the lower note to the pitch of the higher.

VIBRATO: Vibrate the note by rapidly bending and releasing the string with a left-hand finger.

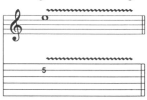

WIDE OR EXAGGERATED VIBRATO: Vibrate the pitch to a greater degree with a left-hand finger or the tremolo bar.

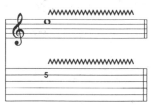

SLIDE: Strike the first note and then with the same left-hand finger move up the string to the second note. The second note is not struck.

SLIDE: Same as above, except the second note is struck.

SLIDE: Slide up to the note indicated from a few frets below.

HAMMER-ON: Strike the first (lower) note, then sound the higher note with another finger by fretting it without picking.

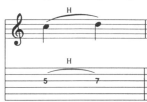

PULL-OFF: Place both fingers on the notes to be sounded. Strike the first (higher) note, then sound the lower note by pulling the finger off the higher note while keeping the lower note fretted.

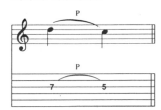

TRILL: Very rapidly alternate between the note indicated and the small note shown in parentheses by hammering on and pulling off.

TAPPING: Hammer ("tap") the fret indicated with the right-hand index or middle finger and pull off to the note fretted by the left hand.

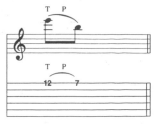

NATURALHARMONIC: With a left-hand finger, lightly touch the string over the fret indicated, then strike it. A chime-like sound is produced.

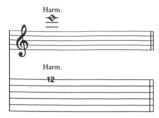

ARTIFICIAL HARMONIC: Fret the note normally and sound the harmonic by adding the right-hand thumb edge or index finger tip to the normal pick attack.

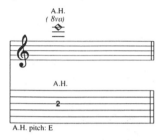

A.H. pitch: E

TREMOLO BAR: Drop the note by the number of steps indicated, then return to original pitch.

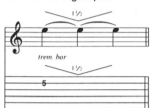

PALM MUTE: With the right hand, partially mute the note by lightly touching the string just before the bridge.

MUFFLED STRINGS: Lay the left hand across the strings without depressing them to the fret-board; strike the strings with the right hand, producing a percussive sound.

PICK SLIDE: Rub the pick edge down the length of the string to produce a scratchy sound.

TREMOLO PICKING: Pick the note as rapidly and continuously as possible.

RHYTHM SLASHES: Strum chords in rhythm indicated. Use chord voicings found in the fingering diagrams at the top of the first page of the transcription.

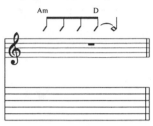

SINGLE-NOTE RHYTHM SLASHES: The circled number above the note name indicates which string to play. When successive notes are played on the same string, only the fret numbers are given.

Definitions of Musical Symbols

Symbol	Definition
8va	•Play an octave higher than written
15ma	•Play two octaves higher than written
loco	•Play as written
pp (pianissimo)	•Very soft
p (piano)	•Soft
mp (mezzo-piano)	•Moderately soft
mf (mezzo-forte)	•Moderately loud
f (forte)	•Loud
ff (fortissimo)	•Very Loud
(accent)	•Accentuate note (play it louder)
(accent)	•Accentuate note with great intensity
(staccato)	•Play note short

Symbol	Definition
	•Repeat previous beat (used for quarter or eighth notes)
	•Repeat previous beat (used for sixteenth notes)
	•Repeat previous measure
	• Repeat measures between repeat signs
	•When a repeated section has different endings, play the first ending only the first time and the second ending only the second time.
D.S. al Coda	•Go back to the sign (𝄋) and play to the measure marked "To Coda," then skip to the section labeled "Coda."
D.C. al Fine	•Go back to the beginning of the song and play until the measue marked "Fine" (end).